Open Wounds

A poetry collection
by m.k. malon

Open wounds

I am ripping off the bandages
On these still bleeding scars
Hoping they will heal more quickly
If I can just let them breathe
If you can just let me be

Death

The dead give no answers
They leave only questions
In their wake
Questions
Questions
And heartache

Catharsis

In the shower
In the darkness
Begging the water
To wash this pain away

Hoping
No, praying

For catharsis

Maybe

Maybe death was better
Maybe death
Was the answer this time

Losing a parent

Admitting that I'm wrong
But it's already too late
Terror creeping in
Will I ever resolve these issues?
Will I ever let go of this guilt?

Spiraling

You were a ledge
On my way to rock bottom
So I held on for too long
Clinging for dear life
Afraid of continuing
To spiral

Sincerity

None of this feels sincere
I have no grief

I am hollow

Nightmares again

It's hard to breathe
And the nightmares won't stop

They're getting worse you know

Playing pretend

I hate it
When you act
Like you don't care
I hate the way
That we pretend

Let me have this

I feel like my life
Doesn't have room
For sadness

Like I'm not allowed
To be sad

Lost in you

I'd rather lose myself
In you
Than lose myself
Alone

Delusional

I was so wrapped up
In the way you made me feel
That I couldn't see
You didn't love me

Destroying myself

I want to kill
All of the parts
Of myself
That weren't
Good enough for you

Me vs. Me

"She died
because that's what people do."

"Yea, well
People also live."

I promise

I already knew
I was broken
I promise you
That I already knew

Insomnia again

This brain
Won't let me sleep
And I am so, so tired

Funeral

How come everyone else
Was crying?

And how come
I wasn't?

3, 2, 1, 0

Three broken hearts
Two sexual assaults
And one dead parent later

And still no word from you

Never understanding

I'll never understand
Why you didn't show up
To the funeral
I'll never understand
How we drifted
So far apart

Begging for a lifeline

Hanging on by a thread
Begging for a life line
Knowing that even with a rope
I'll still have to pull myself in

Too fast again

I always try
To move on too fast
In rebellion against
Holding on for too long

A brave heart

I'm not brave
I'm just used to it
Used to tearing myself open
For everyone else

As if a noose

I dreamt last night
Of shoelaces
And your death

Sneakers meant
For running away
But instead
Tying me down
Tying me to you
And making me drown

Cleaning

Cleaning out your closet
Going through the motions
Of throwing away your clothes
Of throwing away your memory
Completely numb
To the pain I should feel

For you

Cutting myself open
Tearing into my flesh
And putting the worst parts
My worst parts
On display

For you

Losing a parent II

Feeling lost
Not knowing who to turn to
Even though
Everyone is reaching out
Even though
Everyone is trying to help

Not so pretty

This isn't pretty
Or neat

It's just painful
It's just me

To my lifelong "friend"

It upsets me
That you didn't
Reach out
When my mom died

I know we had
Lost touch
But I thought
We were still friends

I guess I was wrong
About you again

Bad guy

How is it
That I'm the bad guy
When I was the one
Trying to defend you

Disappointment

How many more times
Will you disappoint me
Before I stop thinking
That you are perfect

Locked away

There's something traumatic
Locked away
Inside my silence

Drowning myself

Can I drink
Enough booze
To drown out
The memory of you?

Falling apart

And all the pieces
Feel like
They're falling apart

Open wounds II

I thought time
Would heal these wounds
But they keep coming back

Losing a parent III

Learning how to walk
Getting knocked off my feet
And told to pick myself up
Only now a limb is missing
And everyone is acting
As if this is totally normal

Turbulence

These days
We are nothing short
Of turbulent

Actor

I shouldn't expect you
To play the part
I wrote for you
Inside my mind

Emotional chaos

You leave emotional chaos
In your wake
So I am stuck
Fixing myself
And the destruction you caused

You shouldn't have called

Noble Blood

Your father was
The king of giving up
On everything
So it shouldn't have been
So surprising
When you gave up
On me

Would I?

Would I have ever
Lived up to your idea
Of what I should have been?

Would you have actually
Been proud
To have raised
Such a daughter?

Whiskey

Whiskey tastes
Just like
All my ex-boyfriends

Whiskey tastes
Just like you

[Crying]

Vague feelings
Like I'm going to cry
But the tears haven't come out
In over a year
And I wish they would just come
So these feelings could go away

Suffering

I am not willing
To suffer for my art
I have suffered enough
And I write these words
In my attempt to heal

Surviving Winter

The darkness is seeping in
Reminding me of your fire
You always brought the light
You always brought the warmth
And that's how I survived that winter

I'm not sure if I can make it through another one
without you

Losing a parent IV

All my memories
Are wrapped up
In the thought
That you never believed me
When I was telling the truth
And that you never listened
When I needed it most

No memory

I don't remember
My mother's last words to me

Wave of numb

The wave of numb hit
And it didn't leave
Instead of washing away
With the tide
It stayed through the funeral
And for another year after

And it's still here
But it's finally
Starting to fade

Gave up

You gave up on so many things
You gave up on your dreams
You gave up on love
And then finally
You gave up on me

3 years later

The laundry detergent
Finally washed away
The smell of you

Beer

This is the part
Where I try not to
Drown myself
In alcohol

3.13.18

You always helped me
Make sense of my thoughts

Paused

Did I put myself on pause
Waiting for someone
To live up to
The person I pretend you were?

Twice before

After all
We've already been here

But it still hurts the same

Bad habits

Trying to kick
A couple of bad habits
Like hating myself
And falling in love with you

Missing you again

I missed you last night
And I missed you this morning
When I woke up in his bed

Cotton mouth

Putting your words
In my mouth
Shoving them in
Like cotton balls
Until it's full
So that I can't speak
So that I can't breathe

Backlash

I can see on your face
How hurting me
Is your way
Of hurting yourself

Mirror, mirror

I feel like
The person in the mirror
Is not an accurate reflection
Of who I am

Staying too long

I wasn't happy with you
But the thought of not having you
In my life
Was more than I could bear
So I stayed too long

4.7.18

My brain won't stop thinking

Halfway there

I was willing to give up
75% of who I was
If only you would meet me
A quarter of the way
But somehow I was still the one
Asking for too much

Your words

Remember when
I told you
That it was fine
That your words
Didn't hurt me?

Neither do I

Liberated

I was never comfortable
Sitting on your pedestal
My fall from grace
Left me broken
But free

Closeness

I have a problem
With closeness
Both physical
And emotional

Biggest regret

I should've told you
That I loved you
But instead
I walked away
And that regret
Will haunt me
Until my dying breath
Until my dying day

One year

One year later
And look how far I've come

But still no tears

So how am I
Supposed to grieve?

Your shirt

I keep putting on your shirt
And it doesn't smell like you anymore
It's been too long
Far too long

Questions

Why are we both
So afraid
Of hurting each other?

Drive me crazy

Making up stories
Making me feel insane
Making me act insane
Making me be insane

You literally
Drove me crazy

How many words?

How many words
Does it take
To fil an empty heart with sorrow?

Because I'd like to move on

Please do not

Don't point it out
Don't call attention to me
I'm begging you
Please don't make this about me

Lies I tell myself

My brain
Has become too good
At lying to me
About how I feel

4.24.18

I don't know
What happened
To my dreams

I'd be lying

If I said
I wasn't still angry
If I said
I didn't love you anymore
I'd be lying

Oh how I'd be lying

Reasons to stay

Was there ever
A reason
For you to stay with me?

Painful memories

Attempting to write about you
But even the faded memories
Hurts me
More than I can bear

Past tense

When did it get so hard
Just to think about
My past
And what have I
Been running from
All this time

Too many times

I wonder
How many times
I have to tell myself
"he never loved you"
before I will believe it

Repeating myself

Time can't heal these wounds
When I'm repeating
The same patterns
Making the same mistakes
Digging deeper
Into the same scars

With someone else

I don't want you
To be the reason
I'm not meeting someone new
I don't want you
To be stopping me
From falling in love again

Killing the past

I want to kill
The memories
And the problems
That I've caused

I want to stop myself
From damaging you

I want to ruin
The parts of me
That are bad for you

It won't be

It isn't like it was
And it will never be again

Not like that

It isn't as if
It would've worked

It isn't as if
We made any sense

But love never does
Make any sense

Fear of alone

I'm afraid
No one will ever
Love me
Again

And I am terrified
That even if they do
It won't be enough

Lost and afraid

I am so very lost
And so very scared
Of what is ahead

Numb

It's hard
To capture feelings
Inside of words
When you don't have any emotions
Of your own

Now

I didn't know
That I still loved you
And I wish I didn't
Know now

Figuring it out

This is the part
Where I figured out
That we didn't work

Not together
Not ever

Wrinkles

Trying to smooth things over
Slowly realizing
That the relationship
Was more broken
Than it was bent

Not just love

It's not
Just
Love

Sometimes love
Isn't enough

Sometimes
Love
Falls short

I'm fine

I've been playing this part
For so long
That I forgot
That it's just a façade

Not worth it

Sometimes
There just aren't
Any parts
Worth saving

Pushing

I'd like to see
How many times
I can get away with
Pushing you away

Hungry

I am hungry for
What used to be
But unashamed
Of letting go

The person you became
Isn't who
I thought you were

Not grieving

You're the voice in my head
Telling me that
I've never worked hard
A single day of my life
So you'll have to excuse me
If I choose not to grieve

Just not you

Some people
Are worth a broken heart
But you are not one of them

On the floor

The floor was cold
But warmer than her heart
Had ever been

Now II

As if getting over you
Would be easier
The second time around

Searching for you

My soul
Is searching for you
In the dark

Avoiding eye contact

So afraid
Of my soul falling out
Through its own windows

Your name

Your name brings
Instant anger
And I didn't know
I was still mad at you

Reflection

How well
Do you know the person
Staring back at you
From the mirror?

Deserving better

I saw him tearing you apart
Making you cry every day

I was desperately wishing
That you'd realize
That you deserve better
Because you do
Deserve better

Grudges

Trying so hard
Not to hold grudges
Or burn bridges
Because once the ties
Have been cut
There's no putting them
Back together

But why

I don't like
Or trust myself

So why would you?

Actions and words

Actions don't always
Speak louder than words

Which is why he'll never know
How much I loved him

Out of control

And it hurt me too
You know
Each time you lost control

It hurt me too

Afterthought

Always second choice
I am barely visible
Merely
An afterthought

Selfish love

I'm jealous of those
Who allow themselves
To indulge
In self-love

Princess

I wonder if the princess knows
Her loyal knight is courting me

Me
Whom she hath so deemed
Unworthy of affection

Cheating again

You tore each other apart
Taking turns with your cheating
Instead of walking away

Letting go was too hard

Her ex

Goodbye
And good riddance

It only took five minutes
For me to realize
He didn't deserve you
In the first place

In Disney

I made a fool of myself
Defending you
Only for you
To turn around
And take his side

Insulting jokes

You tried to hurt me
With your words
But I took it
As a compliment
Knowing you cared more
About my opinion
Than I did about yours

Have to be

I feel like I have to be everything
Otherwise I run the risk
Of forever being nothing

Reflection II

My reflection and I
Can't seem
To get along

Passive aggressive

Pretending things between us are ok
Turning into passive aggression
And letting our friendship fade

Princess 2

Surrounded by those
Who worship you
Who worship the idea of you
Who worship your facade
Everything you say
Is fake with sweetness
Just sugar-coated lies

After tears

Puffy eyes
After tears
I begged you to leave him

What you want

Do you really
Want to be with a man
Who never chooses you?

Why?

Why couldn't you
Just have been honest
About your feelings?
Maybe we could have
Worked it out
Maybe we could have
Remained friends

Princess 3

Tell me dear princess
Are you happy up there
Atop your high horse
Way up in the tower
As you look down
On your unworthy subjects
Who so blindly follow you
Showering you with love
You know you don't deserve
As you offer nothing in return

November 7th

For some reason
The fact that it's
Not even noon yet
Is making me
Want to kill myself

Thanksgiving Eve

I remember this night last year
Pushing down the thoughts
With alcohol and music
And the noise of other people
All these bodies in the bar
And then staring at myself in the bathroom mirror
But the silence was more than I could possibly bear
And I was too drunk to face myself
To see the reflection
Of who I was that night
So I took a picture of my tits
And I sent it to you
Hoping you would smile
Because I couldn't that night

Work in progress

How long am I allowed
To wear this
"Work in progress"
Sign?

I'm fine II

I have spent
So much time
Pretending to be fine
That I almost
Believed it myself

"he wasn't good enough"

Would you have walked away
Would you have been so upset
If you didn't know
That I was right

First thing

If the first thing
He does each morning
Is make you cry
He isn't worthy of you

Settling for mediocre

Don't settle
For mediocre dates
Out of fear
Of being alone

Like stones

The cracks
And shattered glass
In the window work
Of my soul
Were caused by the words
You threw at me
Like stone

Begin again

I spent years
Running away from this place
How did I end up
Back where I started

In the car

I was the one
Telling the truth
He tried to kiss me in that car
And I pushed him away
I wish that you'd believe me

Never enough

He was never good enough for you
And you should've left sooner
But now that it's all over
I hope your heart can heal

Dirty mouth

This is the part
Where I stop
Unwanted kisses
From men
Who don't deserve me

Me Too

"I'm just trying to make you feel good"
He lied
Over and over
While holding me down
As I pushed him away
Telling him "no"

"But I just want
You to feel good"

Apartment living

And this place feels empty
Hollow
A shell of what
A home should be

Victim

It's not your fault
Even if
You didn't do everything right
It's not your fault
Even if
You feel you made a mistake

It's not your fault
It's not your fault
It's not your fault

Hopeless

But what if there really is no hope?
What if it's actually hopeless?
What then?
Do we cry?
Or do we pick ourselves up
And move on?

Healing process

It took me almost a year
To convince myself
To allow you to convince me
That it was time
For me to start
Healing all these wounds

Meditations

And I was a coward
Who walked away
Too afraid
To uncover these memories
Too afraid
To reveal my demons

Victim II

Even when you do everything right
Bad things can happen
Bad people can happen
Life isn't fair

But you are strong
And you will get through this
And you will move on

Apartment living II

I never finished unpacking
I'll always be ready to leave
Living out of boxes
Is easier
Than calling this place home

Shedding

I am shedding
My outer shell
Of protective numbness

I am raw
Open wounds
Trying to breathe
Trying to heal

Worth it

Trying to shape
This hollow shell
Into someone,
A person,
Worth remembering

Regression

Am I turning back
Into who I was before
All the damage
Or is this something new

Is this healing

Surviving

Some days
Surviving
Is enough

That's enough

Right here

But you're not
As lost
As you seem

Darling
You're right here

Survivor

I have survived
I will continue surviving
Now it is time
To learn to move on
To learn how to live

Finished

And it's been a long road
And the journey's been rough
And I'm not there yet
And I'll never be
Finished

Made in the USA
Columbia, SC
26 December 2018